WORD
ALCHEMY
by Lenore Kandel

Grove Press, Inc.
New York

also by Lenore Kandel:
The Love Book

Library of Congress Catalog Card Number: 67–30112

First Printing

Manufactured in the United States of America

CONTENTS

CIRCUS

POSTER

VENGEFUL EXHIBIT OF ANGELS!
INDECENT EXPOSURE! TRUMPETS!
DANCE OF THE JELLYBEAN GIRLS!

INESCAPABLE PEARL BLOSSOMS
        TORTURE!
        SWEETHEARTS!

        love lyrics of the homesick tiger
        the secret mating dance of
        everybody

        ALL dreams ARE true
        THIS is a dream
        THIS is TRUE

BEAST PARADE

love me, love my elephant . . .
    never mock a tiger
    never tease a lion
    you and your mother
    are kinfolk to the jungle

SEE THE SPANGLED LEOPARD LADY!
watch the elephant ballet, eight thousand pounds of meat
    cavorting
for your languished eye
cumbersome feet used for nefarious purposes
(consider umbrellas in *your* grandma's hollowed foot)
    !WATCH!
    the gorilla takes a leak
    the monkey masturbates
        how life-like . . .
    SEE the
        TIGer
            SWITCH his
            TAIL!
the leopard lady walks her sister on a shining leash
    the eye
    of the tiger
    hides
    behind the sign of scorpio

HERE BE STRANGE BEASTES AND UNKNOWN
LANDES
    HERE BE LIONS
    exhausted
    from the smell of popcorn

high in the altitude of the furthest Everest of benches and
everywhere and down to the very front row seats
the eye of the beast shines from contorted craniums
struggling between homo the human sapiens circa Now and
that dark beast before

turtle-man   sparrow lady
tiger in a dress-suit   monkey in a sweater
beetle-man, ape-man, poodle-man, snake-man, horse-man,
bull-man, camel-man, goat-man, man-man

   !STOP!
   observe your brethren, guard your true love
   these are dark latitudes
   and the ringmaster has wings
   let the parade begin!
   love me, love my elephant . . .
      love my tiger . . .
      love my anything . . .
      get in line . . .

LOVE IN THE MIDDLE OF THE AIR

CATCH ME!
    I love you, I trust you,
    I love you
CATCH ME!
    catch my left foot, my right
    foot, my hand!
    here I am hanging by my teeth
    300 feet up in the air and
CATCH ME!
    here I come, flying without wings,
    no parachute, doing a double triple
    super flip-flop somersault
    RIGHT UP HERE WITHOUT A
    SAFETY NET AND
CATCH ME!
    you caught me!
    I love you!

now it's *your* turn

INVOCATION
AND CLOWNS
DANCE OF
THE BAREBACK RIDERS

eye of newt and heel of brandy
champagne wine and hashish candy
shock of love and touch of madness
demon's tear of final sadness
pulse of vision, blood of stone
kiss of witches, mandrake moan
fear of heaven, bread of dreams
Everything is what it seems

oh! the clowns! but they're beautiful
the ringmaster is clothed entirely in black owl feathers
except for his black suede boots and gauntlets
and his black and braided whip
He flies overhead, circling endlessly
while the clowns pretend to be angels
pretending to be clowns

and the bareback riders . . .
beautiful girls, naked except for silver boots and gloves
their long hair flowing behind them in a luminous wave
all of them, the ones pale and glowing as hot bridal satin
the ones dark as unknown waters   all of them
all of them ride horses white as mist with burning
        sapphire eyes
the horses canter and pace the figures of the dance
tails of seaspray   bodies cool as foam
the beautiful naked girls extend their arms

and weave serene enchantments as they dance
faster and faster
spinning their incandescent shadows into silver fog
that melts, dissolves, and burns
till all that's left transforms itself
into one glittering white and dawn wet rose
that the ringmaster
accepts in trembling hands

FREAK SHOW
AND FINALE

Expose yourself!
Show me your tattooed spine and star-encrusted tongue!
Admit your feral snarl, your bloody jaws
concede your nature and reveal your dreams!
    each beast contains its god, all gods are dreams
    all dreams are true

    LET THE BEAST WALK!!!!
permit the dog to fly, allow the spider love

Are you the rainbow-headed child, the oracle of dream,
the witch of pain, the priest of tears, the door of love?

EXPOSE YOURSELF!
Are you the saint of lust, are you the beast that weeps?

EXPOSE YOURSELF!
Are you BOY 16 WEDS WOMAN 68 shaking with lust
Are you FATHER OF 3 SHOOTS SELF AND INFANT
    SON
Are you MANIAC BURNS LOVERS ALIVE
Are you UNKNOWN WOMAN LEAPS FROM BRIDGE
Are you TEEN-AGE GIRL FOUND CHAINED IN
    ROOM
Are you half-man half-woman, do you weigh six hundred
    pounds, can you
walk on your hands, write with your toes, dance on a
    tight-wire?

11

EXPOSE YOURSELF!

ACCEPT THE CREATURE
AND BEGIN THE DANCE!

INVOCATION FOR MAITREYA

to invoke the divinity in man with the mutual gift of love
with love as animate and bright as breath
the alchemical transfiguration of two separate entities
into one efflorescent deity made manifest in radiant human
    flesh
our bodies whirling through the cosmos, the kiss of heartbeats
the subtle cognizance of hand for hand, and tongue for tongue
the warm moist fabric of the body opening into star-shot rose
    flowers
the dewy cock effulgent as it bursts the star
sweet cunt-mouth of world serpent Ouroboros girding the
    universe
as it takes in its own eternal cock, and cock and cunt united
    join the circle
moving through realms of flesh made fantasy and fantasy
    made flesh
love as a force that melts the skin so that our bodies join
one cell at time
until there is nothing left but the radiant universe
the meteors of light flaming through wordless skies
until there is nothing left but the smell of love
but the taste of love, but the fact of love
until love lies dreaming in the crotch of god. . . .

ENLIGHTENMENT
POEM

we have all been brothers, hermaphroditic as oysters
bestowing our pearls carelessly

no one yet had invented ownership
nor guilt   nor time

we watched the seasons pass, we were as crystalline as snow
and melted gently into newer forms
as stars spun round our heads

we had not learned betrayal

our selves were pearls
irritants transmuted into luster
and offered   carelessly

our pearls became more precious and our sexes static
mutability grew a shell, we devised different languages
new words for new concepts, we invented alarm clocks
fences   loyalty

still . . . even now . . . making a feint at communion
        infinite perceptions
I remember
we have all been brothers
and offer   carelessly

NOW VISION

we all lived (all) together in one (one) house sleeping in our various and separate rooms and I, I woke where I slept, in the arms of one who loved me, leaving four letter words undefined

oh yes I loved port wine warming my belly sweetening my mouth turning on my spirits even more I loved my pot curling incense up my head sliding ashes of laughter out my teeth (attar of roses) riding the vision night   I loved the sun sucking in in through my skin like a miser opening my mouth and my legs for the pretty sunshine loved the cold old fog loved the long wet rain   yet

my best and oldest friend in turning on the world forgot my name and left me hanging paranoid for twenty-seven minutes on an ill-used street with rescue an unasked stranger leading me beyond destruction cities below the earth   embracing me and we made love with each other sinking inexorably below the ground and waking as a bird, all hollow boned living together as we did the house began to change itself   the day we gave up time my room turned golden

once we sat to dinner along the brown and broken table with twelve faces twenty-four hands forty-eight articulated limbs and knives and forks all making motions in the ritual air   the masticating teeth saliva slippage down the long canal and peristalsis little nodule muscles pushing in all the busy bellies I looked around my eyes at fork level and saw eleven sets of hands and one of golden paws taloned feral-clawed bloodstained I was afraid to look up and view what face or lack of one slipped down under the table and through the legs not looking backward and through the curtained doorway out

along the endless dusty hallway I dreamt my door opened into limbo I hung suspended there in nowhere while vampire bats twittered all the empty bed night with the moon burning my window and the wind at my door I could hear the earth turn and the stones crying in the fields and the ice crystals forming and shattering in my body veins my head was an unswept attic a ferris wheel of dust swinging through deserted fair grounds on a rainy night my eyes leaked cobwebs tomorrow I left my room singing chinese love songs out of the stretch of night

oh yes there were days and hours and I have walked this town until I have circled the universe   walking these streets back and forth and hiding in the bird sanctuary house we lived in and I walked down the hall and opened my door into turkish jazz and blew incense over the ceiling and lay down and wept for all the beautiful people now we all (all) lived in this house and there was Maru with her beautiful mississippi bones and her dead baby staring thinly out the window and waiting to jump while her loving lover loved love somehow else and in another land   and there were more (passed out on the kitchen floor drunk again) there were bearded angels hugging scimitars there were unknown soldiers and glory diggers there were zen monks and lovely ladies there were sunflowers in the morning and passing the evening hours I drank blue vervain tea which tasted like bitter flowers like apricot kernels like witch fingers in this house sheltering many passers-by for this world is a bridge they say and it is a long time in crossing and we here ran a tea house with many exits.

oh the night hours the light hours the bright hours all the hours bundled up into each other made such a small package and all we really had

oh yes we are someone else now painting our eyes with the seasons I am a big angel bird squatting in a dark room watch-

ing my feathers grow they burst my skin infinitely   a blind
seraph performing the Indian rope trick on a subway train
   the season has changed the rain has washed away the earth
and the flesh and the bones are whispering white secrets   this
is the bridge this is the bridge and there is
   no   way   back

FAREWELL TO FANCY

Green eyed, white limbed, the libra lady rides straight
down the wind. Nor does she safely sit and wait
for sweet serenity but opens wide for joy
and all devices of delirium she does employ.
Her sea-dawn eyes hold memories of antique Greece
when all the gods came down to kiss and laugh and twine
nor from that lovely loving did they cease
till all that once was human had become divine.

Let there be loving and let the joy run free
Think of this, lady, when you think of me.

WERE-POEM

VISION OF BEASTS!

no man intransigent
but shields the animal within
were-wolf never died
but sits beside you
any time at all

and I have viewed the beast in man

last night I watched a poet glow white at the edges
and his face become that of a tiger

the beast is holy   the man beast is holy
there are directions to go in that have never existed
the man is holy   the tiger-lama invokes the voice of
silence

EXPLOSIONS OF BEING !

the beast burns FIRE on the

HOLY balance waver   FIRE

down the spine the man beast HOLY

in the beginning was   HOLY
in the beginning was   HOLY
in the beginning was   HOLY

and there are existences beyond direction
    HOLY

the mouth of the beast is filled with fire
and he speaks holy

    and in the beginning was what flame-faced totality?

ROSE/VISION

Permit me the concept of the rose
the perfumed labyrinth
that leads one petal at a time
into oblivion's heart

There are visions within the silence of the rose
Here in these velvet rooms accessible to dream
I open my eyes into darkness
until my vision/of itself/ignites the air
and I not only see but am all possibilities
of time and space and change
From which there is no place to hide, no
season of serenity, no solid ground
and Mother Chaos grips my trembling hand
and with *my* fingers tears the veil from her head
and shows me my own pale face
against the sparkling void
and I am bereft of explanations

I am at the turning of the labyrinth
and there is only one direction
and it surrounds me
and I am at the turning of the labyrinth
and there is only one way to go

The rose contains infinity, I hold the rose
and walk within the velvet tunnels of its dream
there is no way to stop or stand
and there is only one way to go

AGE OF CONSENT

I cannot be satisfied until I speak with angels
I require to behold the eye of god
to cast my own being into the cosmos as bait for miracles
to breathe air and spew visions
to unlock that door which stands already open and enter into
    the presence
of that which I cannot imagine

I require answers for which I have not yet learned the ques-
    tions

I demand the access of enlightenment, the permutation into
    the miraculous
the presence of the unendurable light

perhaps in the same way that caterpillars demand their lepi-
    doptera wings
or tadpoles demand their froghood
or the child of man demands his exit
from the safe warm womb

LADY/POEM

ladies with eyes limitless as angels
hover behind white windows
       pale windows
sending their minds over null-time landscapes
incandescent butterflies of breath

    THERE IS NO ROOF TO MY HEAVEN !

lady . . . lady . . . of iridescent dreaming
time is the gesture of your eyelash
         dream of me,
     lady
my brain dances!

will we home to the right bodies, lady
      and will it matter

   THE RAINBOW!

              it breaks   against my eye

   I, rainbow,
   do salute you
or will we giggle   and serve tea
      two hundred years too late

STONEDREAM

name me the sectors of reality, I am no longer sure
time is an invention of the phone company
the universe does not turn off in three minute spurts
clocks are a ploy of the devil

I have dreamed prophecies while wide-awake and found them
      true
    listen!   the honeybee dreams honey and I am awake at
    dawn
    remembering the corridors of dreams unsold
where was the beach on which I found this stone and from
      what mountain
was it washed what hillside knew it first did bee tracks dust
      its surface
was it a glacier gift from alpine tops the world has long forgot
    it fits my hand

EMERALD POEM

there reaches a point without words
    safe   a point deep within the emerald
    seabright washes over eyes and tongue

frozen the stonebirds fly soft among my fingers
their tiny beaks tapping snowflakes from my thumb
        the color of emeralds
the solid becomes the liquid and I the greenbreather
I am at home among the nebulae
      in the heart of the emerald
   safe   a point without words
one is one and I the green breather
      I the gill singer
oh the liquid green flowers that the small birds carry!
   they fade to lavender
     on my tongue
   they fade to lavender on my eyes
oh the stars that devour me in the heart of the emerald
     safe   in the flowers of the emerald
     safe   at the point without words

FIRST THEY
SLAUGHTERED
THE ANGELS

I
First they slaughtered the angels
tying their thin white legs with wire cords
and
opening their silk throats with icy knives
They died fluttering their wings like chickens
and their immortal blood wet the burning earth

we watched from underground
from the gravestones, the crypts
chewing our bony fingers
and
shivering in our piss-stained winding sheets
The seraphs and the cherubim are gone
they have eaten them and cracked their bones for marrow
they have wiped their asses on angel feathers
and now they walk the rubbled streets with
eyes like fire pits

II
who finked on the angels?
who stole the holy grail and hocked it for a jug of wine?
who fucked up Gabriel's golden horn?
             was it an inside job?

who barbecued the lamb of god?
who flushed St. Peter's keys down the mouth of a
North Beach toilet?

who raped St. Mary with a plastic dildo stamped with the
Good Housekeeping seal of approval?
        was it an outside job?

where are our weapons?
where are our bludgeons, our flame throwers, our poison
gas, our hand grenades?
we fumble for our guns and our knees sprout credit cards,
we vomit canceled checks
standing spreadlegged with open sphincters weeping soap suds
from our radioactive eyes
and screaming
for the ultimate rifle
the messianic cannon
the paschal bomb

the bellies of women split open and children rip their
way out with bayonets
spitting blood in the eyes of blind midwives
before impaling themselves on their own swords

the penises of men are become blue steel machine guns,
they ejaculate bullets, they spread death as an orgasm

lovers roll in the bushes tearing at each other's genitals
with iron fingernails

fresh blood is served at health food bars in germ free
paper cups
gulped down by syphilitic club women
in papier-mâché masks
each one the same hand-painted face of Hamlet's mother
at the age of ten

we watch from underground
our eyes like periscopes
flinging our fingers to the dogs for candy bars
in an effort to still their barking
in an effort to keep the peace
in an effort to make friends and influence people

III
we have collapsed our collapsible bomb shelters
we have folded our folding life rafts
and at the count of twelve
they have all disintegrated into piles of rat shit
nourishing the growth of poison flowers
and venus pitcher plants

we huddle underground
hugging our porous chests with mildewed arms
listening to the slow blood drip from our severed veins
lifting the tops of our zippered skulls
to ventilate our brains
            they have murdered our angels

we have sold our bodies and our hours to the curious
we have paid off our childhood in dishwashers and miltown
and rubbed salt upon our bleeding nerves
in the course of searching
            and they have shit upon the open mouth of god
they have hung the saints in straitjackets and they have
tranquilized the prophets
they have denied both christ and cock
and diagnosed buddha as catatonic
they have emasculated the priests and the holy men and

censored even the words of love
    Lobotomy for every man!
and they have nominated a eunuch for president
    Lobotomy for the housewife!
    Lobotomy for the business man!
    Lobotomy for the nursery schools!
and they have murdered the angels

IV
now in the alleyways the androgynes gather swinging their
lepers' bells like censers as they prepare the ritual
rape of god
    the grease that shines their lips is the fat of angels
    the blood that cakes their claws is the blood of angels

they are gathering in the streets and playing dice with
angel eyes
they are casting the last lots of armageddon

V
now in the aftermath of morning
we are rolling away the stones from underground, from the
caves
we have widened our peyote-visioned eyes
and rinsed our mouths with last night's wine
we have caulked the holes in our arms with dust and flung
libations at each other's feet

and we shall enter into the streets and walk among them and
do battle
holding our lean and empty hands upraised
we shall pass among the strangers of the world like a
bitter wind

and our blood will melt iron
and our breath will melt steel
we shall stare face to face with naked eyes
and our tears will make earthquakes
and our wailing will cause mountains to rise and the sun to
    halt

THEY SHALL MURDER NO MORE ANGELS!
        not even us

JOY SONG

My beloved wields his sex
    like a hummingbird
poised on the delicate brink

What pleasure to be a honey plant
       and
    open wide

EROS/POEM

Praise be to young Eros who fucks all the girls!
Only the gods love with such generosity
sharing beatitude with all
Praise be to Eros! who loves only beauty
and finds it everywhere
Eros I have met you and your passing goddesses
wrapped in a haze of lovelust as true as any flower
that blooms its day and then is lost across the wind
I have seen your eyes lambent with delight
as you praised sweet Psyche's beauty with your loving tongue
and then have seen them sparkle with that same deep joy
as other tender ladies lay between your hands
Praise be to Eros! who can hoard no love
but spends it free as water in a golden sieve
sharing his own soft wanton grace
with all who let his presence enter in
faithless as flowers, fickle as the wind-borne butterfly
Praise be to Eros, child of the gods!
who loves only beauty   and finds it
everywhere

HARD CORE LOVE

To Whom It Does Concern

Do you believe me when I say / you're beautiful
I stand here and look at you out of the vision of my eyes
and into the vision of your eyes and I see you and you're an
      animal
and I see you and you're divine and I see you and you're a
      divine animal
and you're beautiful
the divine is not separate from the beast; it is the total crea-
      ture that
transcends itself
the messiah that has been invoked is already here
you are that messiah waiting to be born again into awareness
you are beautiful; we are all beautiful
you are divine; we are all divine
divinity becomes apparent on its own recognition
accept the being that you are   and illuminate yourself
by your own clear light

LOVE-LUST POEM

I want to fuck you
I want to fuck you all the parts and places
I want you all of me

all of me

my mouth is a wet pink cave
your tongue slides serpent in
stirring the inhabited depths
and then your body turns and
then your cock slides in my open mouth
velvety head against my soft pink lips
velvety head against my soft wet-velvet tongue
your cock /hard and strong/ grows stronger, throbs in my
    mouth
rubs against the wet slick walls, my fingers hold you
caress through the sweat damp hair
hold and caress your cock that slides in my mouth
I suck it in, all in, the sweet meat cock in my mouth and
your tongue slips wet and pointed and hot in my cunt
and my legs spread wide and wrap your head down into me

I am not sure where I leave off, where you begin
is there a difference, here in these soft permeable membranes?

you rise and lean over me
and plunge that spit-slick cock into my depth
your mouth is on mine
and the taste on your mouth is of me
and the taste on my mouth is of you

and moaning mouth into mouth

and moaning mouth into mouth

I want you to fuck me
I want you to fuck me all the parts and all the places
I want you all of me

all of me

I want this, I want our bodies sleek with sweat
whispering, biting, sucking
I want the goodness of it, the way it wraps around us
and pulls us incredibly together
I want to come and come and come
with your arms holding me tight against you
I want you to explode that hot spurt of pleasure inside me
and I want to lie there with you
smelling the good smell of fuck that's all over us
and you kiss me with that aching sweetness
and there is no end to love

PEYOTE WALK

1

VISION: that the barriers of time are arbitrary; that nothing
   is still

we, the giants of the river and universe, commencing the act
   of
love, enclosing our bodies in each other's wilderness, vast
   hands
caressing pinnacles of meat, tracing our titan thighs

> one month we touch extremities
> next year a kiss

the giant prick engorged began its downward stroke at years
beginning into years end giant cunt (a) (slow) (sea) (clam)
hips and rotundities earth-moving from month to month and
promises of spring

> orgasmic infinity
> one (!) second long

EARTHQUAKE!
FLOOD!   FLOOD!   FLOOD!

> huge pelvises shuddering
> while worlds burn

2

VISION: that the barriers of form are arbitrary; nothing is still

now   now   now
               moving
tangled my fingers tangle in
      sticky life threads
               moving
between my fingers

a geode, granite walled crystal universe
I see both sides at once
how easy   why didn't I before

       I AM

part of the flow

          the lamp the fig and me
          we the redwoods
          us the walls and winds
               body mine?

  you?
MOTION

beingness   my fingers t–
    angle

the only light our vital glow our radiance
turning to you your face becomes a skull
       MY SKULL!

protean the form encloses space and time
          moving

NOWNOWNOWNOWNOWNOWNOWNOW
NOWNOWNOWNOW

3
VISION: that yes

(we) is (god)

VISION OF THE SKULL
OF THE PROPHET

the bone is not white but yellowed; the skull blown thin
impaled in its entirety upon a staff of witch/wood

from the eyeholes there leaks a slow and steady stream
of minute iridescent crystals
descending like tears against the eroding bone
at the foot of the staff the ground is covered
with tiny crystalline flowers
that bloom only for an instant and then shatter
with the sound of light

in the moment of shattering the prophet-eye
views the universe entire
and dies again to dust

at that moment of sight
any being can share the total vision
any being whose eyes   at that incalculable instant
        are completely open

POEM FOR TYRANTS

sentient beings are numberless—
I vow to enlighten them all
—The First Vow of Buddhism

it seems I must love even you
easier loving the pretty things
the children   the morning-glories
easier   (as compassion grows)
to love the stranger

easy even to realize   (with compassion)
the pain and terror implicit in those
who treat the world around them
with such brutality   such hate

but oh   I am no christ
blessing my executioners
I am no buddha   no saint
nor have I that incandescent strength
of faith illuminated

yet   even so
you are a sentient being
breathing this air
even as I am a sentient being
breathing this air
seeking my own enlightenment
I must seek yours

if I had love enough
if I had faith enough

perhaps I could transcend your path
and alter even that

forgive me, then—
I cannot love you yet

THE FARMER,
THE SAILOR

"I've never seen the ocean . . . "

He stands there, looking out over the green of Wisconsin in
    August

(the spume of barley, the toss of oats, the drift of corn)

"It's a centennial farm—been in the family over a hundred
    years—

my grandpa broke the land—nobody else around here then—
    just him . . ."

It's an island, this place

the farmstead isolate in the high green

Out beyond the barn there's another building

the combine, the mower, rest there

and he strokes their orange bodies carefully

"You gotta have a feel for machinery. I always did. Do a lot of
harvesting for people in this county, the next county, too.
There was a bad hailstorm this year, almost went through
the roof here, see?"

The dents show large in this thick metal roof. The building
itself a ship's hull, joined precisely by his weathered hands.

"Broke all the windows in the house, that hail. Ruined the
    corn.

Planted a second crop though and we'll come out all right, if
    the

weather holds fair."

He pats the combine gently

"No, I've never seen the ocean but I'd sure like to before I
    die.

Got a daughter out in San Francisco and my wife went out
    and visited

her a year ago. She went right *in* the ocean, took off her shoes and
lifted up her skirts and walked right in. Told me it was the prettiest
thing she ever saw."
He stands there, the inland sailor, master mariner of the grassland
and his eye is blue with distance

BUS RIDE

what savage beast would willfully consent to ride jammed
    haunch to haunch
with others of his kind
carried from spot to spot, glimpsing the passing world through
greasy rectangles of heavy glass
    oh god but we are civilized!
  observe the lady, matron-dominant by type
  she wears the uniform: mink coat, silk hat, a small corsage
    of pale
Hawaiian blooms
    no use; old eve still wearing the skins of dead animals
        the genital organs of plants

I remember you, old lady, when you first decided you were
    such hot stuff,
prancing around on your hind legs with that phony apple in
    your teeth—
running on all fours when you thought no one was looking
    (I wonder, do you do that now—I can picture you in
       your
    bar-b-q back yard, stripped down to corset and falsies
    and whinnying at your neighbor's nubile sons with your
    finger up your flabby unsatisfied crotch while your
    de-balled houseman sits inside leafing through playboy
    and swallowing his spit)

again, you and your sisters do surround me, shining the plastic
seats with well-fed bottoms, your arms all crammed with
further goodies for your private delectation
were I that primal beast

I would have torn you joint by joint and saved your bones for
hard nights in the winter for my young to chew on
but civilized
I sit in shame, guarding my own poor bones from such as you
and
leaping from the bus to scurry home, intact
one time again

ANATOMY NOTE

the hand is a flower
space moves the hand through areas of time
    the gesture
blooms and dies

LOVE SONG FOR
SNOW WHITE

in the hollow/of the garden/of the bed/in the crotch
/of the legs/of the tree
where we lie
time descends us like the moss   on an oaktree   on an ash
we grow younger   we grow tender
you and I

BEDSONG
FOR HER

tensions of Rosamond
    the lady fair
destroys herself as deft as any saint
and thirty times a virgin
    beds herself

O lullaby for seven peevish cats!

POEM FOR PETER

God's gentleman can do no wrong
nor right
he moves in grace
which holds no judgment

THREE/LOVE POEM

I stood there with the two men
Kissing first one and then the other
Kissing first one and next the other
While the others laughed in envy and relief
That they didn't have to do it
And that it was being done

MELODY FOR
MARRIED MEN

I like to watch the young girls walk
swinging their hips and hair
swinging their hopes and dreams in magic circles
they never walk alone, but move in twos and threes
confiding audacities to each other
twitching their tails and giggling
while thirty year old men watch from their windows
drinking coffee with their wives and making fantasies
of Moslem heaven

country?   have lost our pride
as nationals   no man can die for billboards
        as have for freedom
who froze his balls at Valley Forge
(14° below) pissed blood and wept in pain
(wept) wept a man willfully engaged
to fight for certain rights

        My brother (34 years old)
drinks chocolate flavored metrecal
writing TV scripts
        My lover (34 years old) catches fine fish
but cannot fill out forms
in triplicate
        (Alaska is not for all of us)
he can barely buy brandy to blur his impotence
he is a man breaking his pride against

What Were Your Earnings Last Year
        and
How Long Have You Lived At This Address
        and
Are You Now

        these men of Gloucester fought arm's length with whales
        (the smell, they say, it never did wear off—
        the reek of such huge dying)
            why be   half safe

yesterday we went to the ocean and prised mussels
from low-tide rocks

cooked them with onion   carrots   celery seed
        (delicious)
cut fingers healed in sea water

there is a pride in handknit sweaters
        unknown
to knitting machines and
            other robots

        Gettysburg was not an outing
        Bull Run, Appomattox, anywhere
        and dance hall girls came high

Fort Sumter   Bunker Hill

THIS IS A NATIONAL MONUMENT

this African student, the other night
        at a party
My people are dying, he said
yaws . . . fevers . . . things like that
I'd like to stay here, he said
direct plays . . .
I must go home and lead my people

SMALL PRAYER FOR FALLING ANGELS

too many of my friends are junkies
too many of my psychic kin tattoo invisible revelations on
    themselves
signing their manifestoes to etheric consciousness with little
hoofprint scars reaching from fingertip to fingertip
a gory religiosity akin to Kali's sacred necklace of fifty human
heads

Kali-Ma, Kali-Mother; Kali-Ma, Kali-Mother
too many of my friends are running out of blood, their veins
are collapsing, it takes them half an hour to get a hit
their blood whispers through their bodies, singing its own
    death chant
in a voice of fire, in a voice of glaciers, in a voice of sand that
    blows
forever
over emptiness

Kali-Ma, remember the giving of life as well as the giving of
    death
        Kali-Ma . . .
Kali-Ma, remember the desire is for enlightenment and not
    oblivion
        Kali-Ma . . .
Kali-Ma, their bones are growing light; help them to fly
Kali-Ma, their eyes burn with the pain of fire; help them that
    they see
with clear sight

Kali-Ma, their blood sings death to them; remind them of life
that they be born once more
that they slide bloody through the gates of yes, that
they relax their hands nor try to stop the movement of the
    flowing now

too many of my friends have fallen into the white heat of the
    only flame
may they fly higher; may there be no end to flight

NAKED I HAVE
KNOWN YOU

naked I have known you
I have watched your face open in the wet heat of love
your mouth of words become hunger and your tongue a
    delicate animal
I have known you

I have known you the skeleton exquisite walking the bright
    red flesh
cocooned in vegetable fiber and plastic and the skins of dead
    animals
moving with careful articulation through forest of concrete
eyeholes anxious at jungle intersections
the blare of sound an imprecation at finger-edge

the only way to walk is one foot in front of the other

        FLY THEN GODDAM YOU!

witch-animal, scurrying to covens underground   rat brother
altar of subway trains   carrier of death capsule immaculate
          V D
        is watching you
oh junkie doorway god-love   the tremor of affliction beating
    your hand
against your other face
I have known you

wind eagle of high land I have seen your fingers elongate and
    burn

I have watched your groin flower
I have known you

naked I have known you I have devoured your head smashed
    through
mirror glass into dimensions uncontrollable I have found you
crystalline guts draped over/across my tongue and eyeballs
    and your
left hand in my stomach and I am digesting it

        the most noticeable thing when falling into the sun
          is
        the exquisite sensation of warmth

sun flower   sunflower dance floor   sunflower radio station
sunflower time bomb   sunflower dog kennel   sunflower
christmas tree   sunflower no trespassing   sunflower
white only   sunflower exit

naked I have known you hiding behind movie sets turning
yourself into holocaust   altar of windwheels
lobotomy dancer I have seen your eyelids nictate lace curtains
I have seen you eight feet high and skinny parading the city
dumps handweaving witch signs
and screaming

NAKED I HAVE SUNFLOWER YOU and the traffic
    backed up for miles
I have watched your face sunflower the eyeholes beds of
    hothouse dirt
and rare plants patterning your cheekbones mouth of sea
    anemone and I
have kissed it
redanimal I have greenplant you   altar of hockshops

and I have seen your face

KIRBY/POEM

I have seen the blue eyes of the centaur
fiery with visions yet unprophesied
    the skull alchemic furnace of the man
        the mind/serpent devouring
        the marrow of the nether bones

    VISION   VISION
    DREAM DESCRIBABLE
PENULTIMATE PROPHECY OF THE BLUE-
    FLAME LOVE/DEATH

Peering beyond and through the eye apertures
I see your skull a geode
Stone shelled kaleidoscope of light

    Within the interior labyrinth of the mind
    the crystal slowly blooms
    transmuting the melted dross
    the soft tissues and decaying bones

THE BEING ITSELF IS THE ONLY SUFFICIENT
    FUEL

Centaur I have known you before me on the zodiac
nudging my heels with your prophetic arrow

Bone bow   bone arrow
gut strung
and with your own untidy guts

Time was I knew you thick with meat
and steady with your years

This day I see your arrow tremble in the sky

JUNK/ANGEL

I have seen the junkie angel winging his devious path over
     cities
his greenblack pinions parting the air with the sound of fog
I have seen him plummet to earth, folding
his feathered bat wings against his narrow flesh
pausing to share the orisons of some ecstatic acolyte
The bone shines through his face
and he exudes the rainbow odor of corruption
his eyes are spirals of green radioactive mist
luminous even in sunlight   even at noon
his footstep is precise, his glance is tender
he has no mouth nor any other feature
but whirling eyes above the glaring faceless face
he never speaks and always understands he answers no one
Radiant with a black green radiance
he extends his hollow fingered hands
blessing   blessing   blessing
his ichorous hollow fingers caressing the shadow of the man
with love and avarice
and Then unfurls his wings and rides the sky like an
enormous Christian bat   and voiceless
flies behind the sun

BLUES FOR SISTER
SALLY

I

    moon-faced baby with cocaine arms
             nineteen summers
             nineteen lovers

      novice of the junkie angel
    lay sister of mankind penitent
        sister in marijuana
        sister in hashish
        sister in morphine

    against the bathroom grimy sink
    pumping her arms full of life
           (holy holy)
she bears the stigma (holy holy) of the raving christ
           (holy holy)
        holy needle
        holy powder
        holy vein

    dear miss lovelorn: my sister makes it with a hunk
    of glass do you think this is normal miss lovelorn

        I DEMAND AN ANSWER!

II

        weep
    for my sister she walks with open veins
    leaving her blood in the sewers of your cities

61

from east coast
to west coast
to nowhere

how shall we canonize our sister who is not quite dead
who fornicates with strangers
who masturbates with needles
who is afraid of the dark and wears her long hair soft and
black
against her bloodless face

III

midnight and the room dream-green and hazy
we are all part of the collage

brother and sister, she leans against the wall
and he, slipping the needle in her painless arm

pale fingers (with love) against the pale arm

IV

children our afternoon is soft, we lean against each other

our stash is in our elbows
our fix is in our heads
god is a junkie and he has sold salvation
for a week's supply

MORNING SONG

Waking in the sweet stale smell of his fond wife's armpit George Vardo remembered realized and regretted the passage of his life, visualizing it as some peculiar bird flapping away past a dreary broad-beamed ferry boat. Where, when, how, he couldn't recall, hadn't noticed, didn't know, only the goneness of it and here he was himself again after an absence of unknowable time.

Eyes shut as an unborn bird he lay unmoving and examined the presence of his wife. wife. WIFE. wiFe. wife. She smelled of moderate talcum powder and pale perfume. Saturday movie theaters. Shoe sweat and popcorn. Undertones of good toast and a rhyme of bacon.

She existed.

Somewhere directly beside him, adjoining his right flank and chest and outflung arm lay a woman. his. wife.

His arm? He flexed the fingers carefully. His arm.

Below him the bed sagged with familiarity. Unyoung. There had been a bed once with gilded frame and orchid colored sheets. great vistas of bedliness. tense springs and eager linen. This bed? NO! never this bed. had been young . . . ever? woven knitted hammered nailed glued and varnish smelling randy legged had sat smug waiting the floor of a department store bounced on by newlyweds with springly heart in price-tag mouth virgin having petted touched felt poked but never DONE THAT THING and sold and carted off and learned the secrets of the night has come to THIS that bed?

He let the hairs on his legs reach out and brush the sheets. They felt gray used until they confided themselves to his body like beaten dogs, cringing spiritless sheets.

63

Wife? His hand was afraid to reach and touch, he flared his nostrils in exploration.

There had been a woman mountain size whom he had wanted with fervid eagerness aching to dive in and excavate, darkest africa with pick and shovel, race up steaming canals, slide all the way up her and out her startled mouth running and making mountain yodels of exhilaration and you can't catch me.

Anxious he felt the balance of the bed and it lay even weight for weight and let his breath come out a little gust of wind. Then not the little girl half-elf come sliding other-world into his hands one street-loose evening when he had been heavy-footed with hunger and hardly looking up and she so soft and small made streetlights into stars.

a little gust of sigh catching his heart he snored ashamed and then ashamed of shame let sighs be sighs.

He reached himself out and his wife rose to him like bread dough, she still asleep and he cringed back a fractured snail and rolling out of bed and naked scurrying through the dusty floor and out the room and never looking once.

And then beyond the door he stood within a narrow hall and dressed himself in black and with a red rose in his hand went out into the real world.

and opened up his eyes.

The street was long enough and he was wide enough and George Vardo woke up in the familiar warmth of his wife's body and they performed an act of fornication and shared nothing for breakfast and George dressed himself and went to work

feeling. somewhere.

a faint disturbing sense of loss.

TELEPHONE FROM
A MADHOUSE

the way it happens, I'm sitting here in this semi-secure four-
walled building
there is the cool texture of a wooden floor under my naked
feet
and I'm drinking black coffee
from a pretty rice bowl that curves my hands
when the phone rings
and when I lift that dark plastic instrument and put it to my
ear, put it to my carelessly hello-ing mouth
this voice from a million miles away, from a treeless plain,
from a gray wet dank abyss
comes out to me
Are you there? it says, the anxiety of it cutting my calm like a
spiritual buzz saw
Are you there? Are you *really* there? Sometimes I can't believe
you exist, are you there, are you there, really there?
Yes, I murmur, yes yes yes, gripping at the floor with my bare
brown toes, rubbing my sweaty fingers against the wall
Yes, I murmur, yes yes yes   counterpoint to the soft and
desperate tears that drip over the phone at me
Yes, I say firmly, snapping my voice like a lion whip, I'm here
I'm here I REALLY EXIST
and my hands wandering the wall, rubbing my tense muscled
thigh, spreading themselves before my analytic eyes
Yes, I murmur, yes, yes, yes

Later I pass behind the polite and sterile madhouse walls
flashing my visitor look at the fish-eyed nurses

and padding down the barren corridor to room on the left
    number seven
where the voice lies waiting
tangled in soiled bedclothes her   old woman slow
feral eyes break at me   shuffle walking
among the tears the   up and down
darkened room she   the hall
leans up stares at   all the time
me arrowing my soul   all the time
the voice sobs at me
YOU CAME   oh i
can't go on i can't
i don't want to live
any more   and tears
blossom reblossom
man-eating flowers out of
the puffy gray-green eye   shuffle up
sockets   they eat up her   and down the
swollen face   WHAT AM I   corridor
GOING TO DO   up and down
I wiggle up onto the thin   up and down
and high and narrow bed
utterly wordless I reach
out arm around the pale
body in split back
hospital sackcloth and
head against my shoulder
she SCREAMS
and nurse ambulances up
sirening   one foot drags
as I whisper it's all right
trying to push the words
out through my fingers

66

on her shaky back   and
fixing nurse with
glaring eyes until she
drifts away in
starched disorder
showering me with
distrust   but
going
I whisper whisper it's
all right   until the
sobbing softens and
her sad head lifts
and questions me
again
it *is* all right   I
whisper and
thank you   she
whispers back
but is it?   and
I am speechless
pull out one small
gray pigeon feather
I found lying on
the steps of
the hospital
and offer it
she takes and
strokes it, nodding
her head
pigeons are real   it
seems
thank you she whispers
again   and

visitors pass by
furtively
wearing outdoor
faces and peering
into the rooms
as if they were
keyholes

the room is
small the walls
are enema yellow
the shade is down
the light is off
it could be any
hour in the world

GODDAM IT   you
think I'll stand
for this well I
won't I'll show
you all you bloody
jackasses   screams
next door

67

we keep nodding
two windy figures
in a Chinese gale
Are you all right
she asks
It's a beautiful day I
answer the sun is
blooming the flower I
found roses on the
sidewalk
in North Beach
(nodding)
we had a party last
night I had tea cakes
for lunch how are
you
Terrible, she nods
terrible
i don't think i'll
ever get well
i'm afraid
they want me to get
out of bed
and i can't
i smell bad
the world is
disintegrating and
i don't have
anything to hold
on to

and she is trembling
in the terrible wind

old woman up and
down the corridor
all the time
all the time

face peers in the
room and
                    goes
                          away

up and down
up and down

right foot drags

HELP a voice
calls piteously
help   help
help

the tears are
gobbling her eyelids
nobody will ever
love me   she sighs
i am afraid   i am
afraid of everything
terrible she nods
terrible
I kiss her tears like
january sleet touch
my mouth and
I go away

help

VISITING HOURS

ARE NOW

OVER

IN TRANSIT

Question: Locate the center of infinity
Answer: Anywhere

IT   NEVER   STOPS   MOVING!

The ceaseless alchemical permutation, gold into history,
rain into strawberries, strawberries into my bloodstream,
my blood into flowering dreams

the dream into absolute perception, into coruscating visions of
THIS IS WHERE IT IS BA–BY into
infinity

It is necessary to search the spirit through the light of one's
own bioluminescence

THERE IS NO SUCH THING AS STANDING STILL

The balance is that of a gyroscope, motion existing within
        motion
the balance of a bird listening to its heartbeat
wings poised against the currents of the air, eyes tracing the
turning of the earth, the planet circling the sun, the sun
        spinning
its golden path in the universe, and the universe breeding
        life and
death in infinity

and the bird hangs halfway up the sky
infinite motion   at rest   within infinite motion

70

LET IT GO!

"Whatever you see that is beautiful
    don't hang on to it
whatever you see that is terrible
    don't hang on to it"

LET IT GO!

The balance is that of sunlight on water
the sunlight moving as the earth turns, the water
following its gravity path into eventual raindrops
and home to another river
the sunlight-and-water being one and together for the
    duration
of their parallel flow

there is no way to stop water
if you lock it up it will evaporate and reach the clouds
    anyhow
there is no way to stop the sun
it holds its own galactic balance and moves
according to the nebulae of outer space

LET IT GO!

IT   NEVER   STOPS   MOVING

there is movement within a mountain
a rock, a thought, a flower, a light bulb,
a cat, a star, a rice bowl, an arrow

LET IT GO!

71

IT NEVER STOPS MOVING

there is no such thing as standing still
the direction of motion is frequently a matter of choice
when you try to stop other things from moving
you give yourself an impetus toward backwards motion

LET IT GO !

Most of the time
   you will be the *it*
being let go of

IN THE COMICS

last night I saw the holy trinity
      Superman, Batman, and Robin
they were shooting it up in my bathroom
when I came home from a hard day's dreaming
OH POP! OH ZAP!
Superman alone did up 700 ccs of POW!

Later we traded secrets
I told them nothing and they told me all

     there are only ten real people left outside the comics
     everyone else is a Martian
          or a hero
   or a robot programed to think he is a hero
          or you

       WHAM! well pop my zowie, dad, who would have
          dreamt
       that Superman was really the Panchan Lama, and
          sitting
       right next to me here at school!

Captain Marvel is your mother

       (I suppose you wonder why I came to you in
       the garb of an Egyptian temple dancer of
       nearly two thousand years ago)

  POW! WHAMMMMMM! OH ZOWIE ZOWIE
  ZOWIE

Batman makes it with Robin
Robin makes it with eagles
Superman never does

BAM! BAM! THUD! CRAAAACK!

(to others it looks as if the positioning of her arms
is part of a dance but to me her arms are signaling
information in semaphore)

    Superman is a Martian in drag! ZOOOOOOM!
    Wonder Woman is Superman in drag! ZIIIIP!

DRAG! DRAG! DRAG!   ZIP! ZIP! ZIP!

        (helpless in the clutches of the awesome
        monster from another time Batman rolled
        up his sleeve and shot up three thousand
        ccs of WHAM!)

(I weigh only ninety-eight pounds—yet I can
paralyze a 200 pound attacker with just a finger—
because I know   VAZAAAAAAAAAAP!)

      oh SCRUUUUNCH, baby, we can't go on this way
          any longer,
      there must be a way out of this costume!

      KA—WHAMPF!

CRANNNNNNNG!   BLAM! BLAM! BLAM!

    Dad! Superman stands for law, justice, and order!
    Why is he acting like a tyrant?

Pffffff! Click! Hmmmmmmmmmm!

Search on! Search all you want! The only way
you'll ever find it is with the help of these
magic mushrooms!

BAM! BAM!
THUD!

Time's running out fast! If only the clock
would stop ticking . . .

ZIP! POP! WOWIE!

then I'm no longer a super-hero but
just another broken down old has-been

WE ARE ALL EQUALLY INVINCIBLE!

WOW!   WOW!   WOOOOOOOW!

HOROSCOPE

!FIRE!

this is the day all library books become due

!FIRE!

this is the day the sewers break and the gas is shut off

!FIRE!

this is the ohglorygod listen to the song of the white-crowned
    sparrow outside my narrow citystreet window outside
    my narrow night and heartache

!FIRE!

you are kind, obedient, thoughtful, and a pederast

!FIRE!

Orphan Annie has a controlled habit
                                    so does her dog

!FIRE!

you are going on a long trip
you are not going on a long trip
you are going to get busted by a spaghetti-eating cop and
    sentenced
to nine years in a tract house scrawling HELP on the win-
    dows with
a broken enema tube

76

!FIRE!

you are going to eat a tall dark man

!FIRE!

(how many times have I told you to put a
newspaper under your feet when you lie down
on the couch I mean after all you could show
a little consideration)

!FIRE!

(I'd buy your painting but the color just
doesn't go with my new living room set do
you have one with more red in it??)

!FIRE!

your fly is unzipped

!FIRE!

wouldn't you be happier with your own people

!FIRE!

there is no forecast for tomorrow

!FIIIIIIIIIIIIIIIIIIIRE!

POEM FOR PERVERTS

Come be my leather love!
and hand in glove we'll play our own amazing games
behind locked doors and silent window shades

> But she's exquisite!
> Six and a half inch high black patent leather boots
> that lace up tightly to the tender crotch, a brass and
> leather belt of chastity, a French-made corset that
> laces sixteen inches small, black leather gloves from
> fingernail to armpit (so tight it took an hour to ease
> them on), and best of all, a featureless black leather
> hood fitting over the entire head and gathered
> snugly at the neck permitting (exquisite!) only des-
> perate painful breathing and no movement whatso-
> ever

Be mine! Be mine!
I'll buy you iron fetters for your tiny wrists!

> The Fat Man, completely naked except for black
> leather gloves, made a gesture and they removed the
> hood leaving only a thick blindfold. They forced her to
> her knees in front of him and he put his gloved hands
> on her head and giggled softly as he pushed it where
> he wanted it. There was nothing she could do except
> obey.

I'll buy you manacles and thongs
and lash you trembling to the chairs
I'll lead you at midnight on a dog chain

to secret parties where Lady Olga demands *discipline*
and even I am subject to her whims

Exotic ladies!
Members of CLUB UNUSUAL!
Heroines of the spanking brigade
Heroes in lace-trimmed silken underwear, subjected to
            UNSPEAKABLE INDIGNITIES!

Virgins of thirty-six with elongated tongues and clawlike nails
        Affectionate young man, accustomed to discipline and
        fond of frolic
        Will cook and clean, desires only good home and a
        STERN MISTRESS
        UNSPEAKABLE INDIGNITIES!

Come be my bondage queen!
We'll meet on Friday afternoons and play
"Who'll Wield the Whip" and "Hide the Dildo"
you'll count to ten and find yourself in any one of seventy
        predicaments

                Bound To Please!

            The bride wore black leather and carried a neat
            bouquet of riding whips; the groom donned a French
            maid's costume and was given away by Madame
            Tyrant of the well-known Tyrant Boarding Acad-
            emy. The nuptials were celebrated by the Fat Man,
            who accepted the caudal kiss from all participants
            at the close of the ceremonies.

Love, he whispered, Love is my whip
and etched his ardor on her slender back

The blood wreathed down like roses!
until she wept for joy who also wept for pain

Behold the fantasy of man gone civilized!
No naked brute could dream these delicate deceits
   "Be mean to me," he begged
   "No," she said, "I won't, I won't do it"
   "Ah," he sighed ecstatically,
   "I knew that you'd be mean"

"Lick it!" demanded Madame Olga, and Poor Francine com-
plied, the tears running down her tender cheeks

"Lick it!" demanded the Fat Man, and Poor Evelyn obeyed.
She was chained on hands and knees but she lifted her head
obediently, her blue eyes overflowing with tears

"Lick it!" ordered Nina, the French Maid, and Poor Harry did
as she said, having learned the folly of rebellion at the cruel
hands of Madame Tyrant

Lick it! Adore the booted foot, the gloved hand, the whip, the
rod, the Agony Pear, the manacles, the chains, the Witches'
Cradle, and the spanking board!
There is no way out, each door a further entrance to new
indignities and epicurean conceits of anguish impossible to
dream on, the carnivorous bloom of flowering neurosis gone to
synthetic seed.
There are no exits in Bondageland, there is no way back!

   Exquisite! breathed the Fat Man
   He adjusted his pallid bulk delicately
   and mounted the blue-eyed corpse

80